Developing Writing Fluency
Hundreds of Motivational Prompts

Written by
June Hetzel and Deborah McIntire

Editor: Alaska Hults
Illustrator: Corbin Hillam
Cover Photographer: Michael Jarrett
Designer: Terri Lamadrid
Cover Designer: Moonhee Pak
Art Director: Tom Cochrane
Project Director: Carolea Williams

CTP © 2000 Creative Teaching Press, Inc., Huntington Beach, CA 92649
Reproduction of activities in any manner for use in the classroom and not for commercial sale is permissible.
Reproduction of these materials for an entire school or for a school system is strictly prohibited.

Table of Contents

Introduction

Teachers approach the instruction of writing with the purpose of helping children in three areas: fluency, form, and mechanics. The focus of this book is fluency. The prompts are organized around essential aspects of the four writing domains, including skill concepts and writing products (e.g., persuasive essay, campaign speech, friendly letter). Critical components of form are included on each page. This book can be used independently or in conjunction with a regular writing program. The prompts provide students with many choices for Continuous Daily Writing (CDW).

Continuous Daily Writing

Just as children become better readers by reading, so children become better authors by writing. Fifteen to twenty minutes of daily, non-stop writing provides frequency of practice. Each CDW entry is a rush of spontaneous ideas—much like a brainstorm, but in narrative text. The writing is continuous and connected. Students' pencils should never stop moving. Students do not stop to correct mechanics, cross out, or rewrite. Stopping for mechanical corrections and revisions may inhibit the free flow of thought.

Organization of Domains and Writing Prompts

There are 52 weeks of writing ideas to choose from, organized into 13-week segments by the four writing domains: expressive, narrative, informative, and persuasive. Each week has six writing prompts with a particular focus (e.g., short story, advertisements), a wild-card prompt (not related to the focus), and one free-choice selection. The order of topics does not matter; however, if you have been emphasizing a particular writing product (e.g., persuasive essays), you may wish to use the prompts listed under that product.

Each domain begins with a one-page introduction that highlights student background knowledge, career application, and making the most of the writing process. This page also includes teacher tips. Domains can be covered in any order, but starting with the expressive domain will lay a strong foundation in literary devices that will benefit student writing in all domains.

Topic Choice

Do not assign topics to students. Instead, give students a page of topics from which to choose. Invite them to select topics in any order or write on one topic for a few days or even the entire week. If a student is not interested in any of the topics listed, encourage him or her to create another topic of interest (free choice) or respond to recent literature he or she has read. The most important aspects of CDW are that students have access to an interesting topic and that the teacher provides time for students to develop continuous, fluent writing in an uninterrupted atmosphere.

Many students discover that one writing prompt leads to a rather lengthy piece, and they may wish to continue their writing beyond the 15-minute CDW or into the next day's CDW time. Give students the freedom to continue writing on topics of interest during a writing period, at home, or during free time. Encourage continuous exploration of ideas even when some drafts may never be completed. C. S. Lewis said that some of his best books were based upon notes and manuscripts written several years previously and then revisited.

Students who write on topics that interest them will be much more inclined to develop enthusiasm, motivation, and positive attitudes towards writing. So, if one student keeps choosing science topics, encourage him or her to do this—in all likelihood, these strong preferences predict later career goals. Help set the stage for the enjoyment of writing.

Materials and Daily Procedure

Each week provide students with one sheet of ideas that coordinate with your writing program. Have them write their name and the date of the first day of that week at the top of the page. Have students initial or cross off the box next to each prompt to which they respond. At the end of the week, ask students to staple the sheet to the papers they generated, and have them store these papers in a CDW folder. Encourage students to revisit these papers if they would like to further develop any of the topics at a later time.

Have students choose their topic prior to a recess or lunch break and then participate in CDW right after the break. The break time provides a gestation period prior to the writing session. Have students place a topic sheet, a notebook, and two or three sharpened pencils on their desk when they leave for break (so they do not need to get out of their seat to retrieve writing utensils during CDW). When students reenter the classroom, have them immediately go to their desk to write. Similar to Sustained Silent Reading (SSR), have students stay on task during CDW and focus on their writing. If you cannot provide students with this break, consider lengthening the CDW time by an additional five minutes. Set a timer, and encourage students to use the five minutes before the timer rings to think about their topic. When the bell rings, have students begin writing.

A Balanced Writing Program

A balanced writing program incorporates time for teaching fluency, form, and mechanics. Continuous Daily Writing provides an opportunity for students to develop and experience writing *fluency*. Introduce *form* during direct instruction on the structure and framework of each writing topic. Students will strengthen or reinforce form as they make knowledgeable revisions of their writing based on the required format of their writing product and an understanding of the key characteristics of good writing in a particular genre. For example, a friendly letter requires the date, greeting, body, and closing, while an essay requires an interesting lead, details, and a strong ending. *Mechanics* refers to grammar, punctuation, and spelling. Students refine mechanics during the editing process. Time spent in all three areas helps authors develop their skills to their fullest potential.

It may be that students will begin writing products during CDW that they will want to revise later for larger writing projects. Great! However, during the confines of CDW, students should still be expected to "push the envelope" in their writing fluency. Revising, editing, and publishing should be reserved for later. CDW time is exclusively for continuous flow of thought on paper. CDW promotes the brainstorming and rough draft stages of the writing process. Revision, editing, and publishing can be saved for your writing program.

There are a million ways to elicit interest in the subject of writing. Let your creative juices flow ... and also those of your students. Invite them to enjoy, explore, and freely write as they develop a high degree of fluency. Over time you will guide the development of form and mechanics within the context of your writing program. However, for some part of the school day, every student needs to experience the pleasure of simply writing.

Assessment and Lesson Planning

Once a week collect samples of student writing and assess how the class as a whole is meeting the critical components of each week's writing concept or product. Lead a class discussion the following day to share your discoveries. Do not refer to specific student papers because the papers are not meant to be assessment tools for the growth of any one student. Instead, discuss patterns you identified in the samples to encourage students to consider and develop their use of the critical components for that week's writing. In addition, use the samples to help guide your understanding of the skills of the class as a whole. For example, it may become clear that the class needs to develop its understanding of organization, focus, or a particular element of grammar or punctuation. Use this information to help you plan your lessons within the context of your writing program. Do not, however, use the papers generated from CDW as examples. You do not want to encourage students to focus on editing during the fluency practice of CDW. Return samples to students by the end of the week to be filed with that week's papers.

Invite students to assess their own interest and performance in writing with the Self-Survey I reproducible (page 7). Distribute the Self-Survey I reproducible at the beginning of the school year, and invite students to answer the questions honestly. Collect the surveys, and use them as a springboard to discussion or to guide curriculum choices without referring to individual comments or surveys. At the beginning of the next semester, distribute the Self-Survey II reproducible (page 8), invite students to reflect on their growth thus far, and encourage them to answer the questions honestly again. Then, distribute the first self-survey, and encourage students to compare their answers. Finally, help students set goals for the upcoming semester.

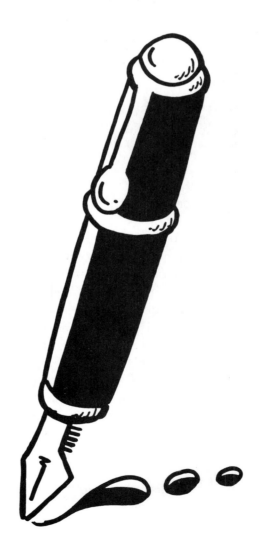

Author _____   Date _____

Self-Survey I

Directions: Answer questions 1–6. Use this scale to answer questions 1, 2, and 3:

1	2	3	4	5
Not at all		Somewhat		Extremely

1. On a scale of 1 to 5, how much do you enjoy writing? _____

2. On a scale of 1 to 5, how well do you feel you write? _____

3. On a scale of 1 to 5, how important do you think it is to write well? _____

4. Do you write for your own pleasure outside of class? _____

5. What kinds of writing do you enjoy the most (e.g., letter, story, report)? _____
   _____
   _____

6. If you had free time to write about topics of your choice each day, how many minutes would you like to write on self-selected topics (e.g., ten minutes, fifteen minutes)? _____

Author _____   Date _____

Self-Survey II

Directions: Answer questions 1–9. Compare the answers to the first six questions to those on your first self-survey. Then, write on the back of this sheet three to five goals you have for your own writing and a sentence for each describing how you might achieve those goals. Use this scale to answer questions 1, 2, and 3:

1	2	3	4	5
Not at all		Somewhat		Extremely

1. On a scale of 1 to 5, how much do you enjoy writing? _____

2. On a scale of 1 to 5, how well do you feel you write? _____

3. On a scale of 1 to 5, how important do you think it is to write well? _____

4. Do you write for your own pleasure outside of class? _____

5. What kinds of writing do you enjoy the most (e.g., letter, story, report)? _____
   _____
   _____

6. If you had free time to write about topics of your choice each day, how many minutes would you like to write on self-selected topics (e.g., ten minutes, fifteen minutes)? _____

7. Which topics on which you wrote recently were most interesting to you? _____
   _____
   _____

8. What kind of progress do you feel you have made in your writing so far this year? _____
   _____
   _____

9. How do the prompts help or hinder you? _____
   _____
   _____

Developing Writing Fluency © 2000 Creative Teaching Press

The Expressive Writing Domain

The expressive writing domain contains products such as poetry, friendly letters, and journals. To write effectively in the expressive domain, students must master literary devices, including sensory detail, alliteration, simile, and metaphor. Provide students with a foundation for writing effectively across the curriculum by teaching them to write material that is vivid, descriptive, stimulating, and inspiring or in some way evokes emotion or inspires action from the reader.

Student Background Knowledge

Tap into students' background knowledge by learning about their interests, emotions, and responses to the world around them. For example, you can explore background vocabulary by having students create group word banks that reflect their responses to a beautiful sunset, a starry night, or an ominous thunderhead. As students write verbs, nouns, and adjectives related to these aspects of nature, you become increasingly familiar with their personal vocabulary. Having students brainstorm vocabulary banks prior to CDW is one way to provide reluctant authors with a place to start.

Career Application

Everyone needs to write for some part of his or her job. Clarity is essential. Representing ourselves well on paper may make or break a career. Throughout your writing lessons and CDW, emphasize to students the importance of audience. Tell students that in any writing situation, they must be keenly aware of the reader. Direct students to keep the audience in mind when selecting appropriate vocabulary. Have students identify the audience when they choose their prompts.

Making the Most of the Writing Process

Have student or parent volunteers cut out interesting pictures from travel magazines and other periodicals. Have them use spray glue to carefully mount these pictures on construction paper. Laminate the mounted pictures for durability. Keep them in file folders organized by topic for easy retrieval and frequent use. The photographs can provide an easy springboard for a student whose imagination needs igniting. For example, perhaps you have assigned writing prompts for Olfactory Sensory Detail (page 14), and you have a student who is not interested in any of the prompts. Invite him or her to choose a picture from the file of foods and his or her creative juices will immediately begin to flow.

The Mind's Eye
Critical Components of Visual Sensory Detail

- Use words and phrases that vividly describe the sense of sight (e.g., *Clear skies and bright sunshine melt the snow, revealing the leafless branches of the surrounding forests*).
- Use specific nouns to replace common nouns (e.g., *tulips* instead of *flowers*).

☐ Brainstorm descriptive adjectives for the following subjects: a baby lion cub, a deserted cabin, and an erupting volcano. Choose one subject and use your adjectives to write a "word picture."

☐ Frances Hodgson Burnett had a garden of 300 rosebushes at her home in England. This was her favorite place on earth and where she was inspired to write *The Secret Garden*. Describe your favorite location and explain why this place is so special.

☐ Brainstorm as many concrete nouns (objects, not ideas) as you can for items you might find in one or more of the following places: a deserted island, a crowded city, an amusement park, and a meadow in springtime. Choose one place and use your concrete nouns to write a descriptive paragraph.

☐ Use an imaginary zoom lens to write a word picture. Describe your school, starting with a long shot, and then zoom in to provide visual detail for a specific area, such as the playground or the library.

☐ Think of your favorite holiday. Write a paragraph describing how you and your family celebrate it. Use concrete nouns and descriptive phrases to write a word picture of your celebration.

☐ Think back to a special time you recently experienced (e.g., a picnic, a party, or a shopping spree). Record the emotions you had during this event. Write a paragraph that captures these emotions

☐ **Wild Card:** What are four animals you would not want to be? Explain your answer.

☐ **Free Choice**

Hear Ye! Hear Ye!
Critical Components of Auditory Sensory Detail

- Use words and phrases that vividly describe the sense of sound (e.g., *The child's sobs pierced the heart of her mother*).

- Use onomatopoeia—words that sound similar to the sound they describe (e.g., *swish, bark, thump*).

☐ Use several of the following onomatopoeic words in a paragraph describing the sounds you hear at a basketball game: *dribble, stomp, creak, thump, swish, roar.*

☐ Michelangelo, the Italian artist and sculptor, spent more than four years on a scaffold, head bent back, 60 feet in the air, painting the enormous ceiling design of the Sistine Chapel at the Vatican in Rome. Imagine that you are Michelangelo. What sounds would you hear around you, or from the people below you, in the enormous church?

☐ Think of your favorite amusement park. List the sounds you might hear if you stayed at the park from opening to closing. What activities are associated with these sounds?

☐ You are alone—lost in a vast rain forest. There is no moon and everything around you is pitch black. You can see nothing, but your ears are exploding with sounds. Describe what you hear.

☐ Choose several of your favorite colors. Brainstorm sounds that represent each color (e.g., *White sounds like snowflakes drifting from the sky. Red sounds like drums beating wildly*).

☐ You are a pet spider brought to school by your owner in a matchbox, which has been shoved inside a pocket. It is lunchtime and you find yourself in the cafeteria. Describe the sounds you hear.

☐ **Wild Card:** Jackie Robinson was the first African American baseball player to play on a major team, the Brooklyn Dodgers. The theme of his whole life was breaking down barriers between people. If you could break down any barrier in the world today, what would it be? Why?

☐ **Free Choice**

Developing Writing Fluency © 2000 Creative Teaching Press

Pleasing to the Touch
Critical Component of Tactile Sensory Detail

- Use words and phrases that vividly describe the sense of touch (e.g., *The coarse, scorching-hot sand scalded the child's tender feet*).

☐ You have been given the assignment of designing the costumes for a Halloween party. What costumes would you design? What textures and fabrics would you use for each costume?

☐ Brainstorm as many words as you can to describe textures (e.g., *smooth, sticky*). Next brainstorm as many items as you can for each word (e.g., sticky: *chewed gum, sucker, molasses*).

☐ Would you prefer to live in a cold climate like Alaska or in a hot, humid climate like the Amazon Rain Forest? Write a descriptive paragraph about the climate of your choice. Be sure to include details about the weather and its effects.

☐ List your family members. Brainstorm words and phrases that describe the tactile sensory details you associate with each of them (e.g., *Grandmother: smooth, silky texture of her satin couch, Grandfather: scratchy, prickly beard*).

☐ You have been blindfolded and led into your classroom. You must identify familiar objects through handling them. Describe the textures and surfaces you encounter.

☐ You are deep-sea diving. You start at the surface of the ocean and descend to the ocean's depths. Describe what you experience along the way. Describe the textures of the coral reef, the sea plants, and the various shells and rocks. If you were able to touch the fish and sea creatures, what would they feel like?

☐ **Wild Card:** Invent a school of the future that your children would like to attend. What would be the same? What would be different?

☐ **Free Choice**

Developing Writing Fluency © 2000 Creative Teaching Press

Author _____ Week Beginning _____

Taste Buds
Critical Component of Taste Sensory Detail

- Use words and phrases that vividly describe the sense of taste (e.g., *As I bit into the cookie, the delectable taste of chocolate exploded in my mouth*).

☐ Create five new flavors of ice cream. Describe how they taste. Are they similar to existing flavors? How do they differ?

☐ You have been invited into the kitchen of a master chef who has prepared all of your favorite foods. Describe what he or she has prepared and the taste sensations you experience.

☐ Brainstorm foods that are chewy, bitter, salty, rough, crunchy, and sweet. Next, pick your favorite category and write a commercial describing these foods. Use descriptive words and phrases to convince your listeners how delectable these items are.

☐ What is the one food you would most like to eat every day of your life? Describe its taste in such a way that you could convince others to join you.

☐ Brainstorm words that describe the way things taste (e.g., *salty, sweet, spicy*) and ways to taste (e.g., *slurp, gulp, gobble*). Write a descriptive paragraph about a boy or girl your age who has discovered a food fantasyland and spends 24 hours tasting a variety of wonderful foods—without getting sick. Use as many of your brainstormed words as possible.

☐ Babe Ruth, the legendary baseball player, ate pickled eels (made by Lou Gehrig's mother) with chocolate ice cream before games. What is the most unusual food combination you have ever eaten? Describe this taste sensation in detail.

☐ **Wild Card:** Wolfgang Amadeus Mozart loved animals and had many pets, including a dog, various birds, and a grasshopper. Write about your favorite pet or a pet you would like to own.

☐ **Free Choice**

Aromatic Feast
Critical Component of Olfactory Sensory Detail

- Use words and phrases that vividly describe the sense of smell (e.g., *The aroma of hot buttery popcorn filled the air*).

☐ Brainstorm pleasant and unpleasant smells.

☐ Brainstorm smells that are associated with one or more of the following scenes: a campfire, a locker room after a game, your kitchen on Thanksgiving.

☐ Johann Sebastian Bach, the beloved German organist and composer, loved good food. He once wrote an entire cantata (song) about coffee and stated that he liked the aroma as much as the taste. What are some of your favorite smells? What pleasurable activities do you associate with them? What emotions do these smells bring up?

☐ Brainstorm the major holidays and celebrations you and your family observe. Next, list some of the scents and aromas you associate with each holiday. Choose one celebration and write a paragraph describing your activities and the aromatic treats associated with them.

☐ What is the worst odor you have ever smelled? Write about where you smelled this, what you did, and how you felt.

☐ List your favorite colors. Brainstorm smells that you associate with each color (e.g., *red: fire, spiced cinnamon apples*). Use these color/aroma combinations in a short descriptive paragraph or poem.

☐ **Wild Card:** If you could grant your best friend three wishes, what would they be? Give reasons for your answers.

☐ **Free Choice**

Author _____ Week Beginning _____

Sound Sensations
Critical Component of Alliteration

- Include a series of words that begin with the same sound (e.g., *busy, buzzing bees*).

☐ Choose several letters of the alphabet. Brainstorm words that start with the sound of each letter. Then, create alliterative sentences from your word groupings (e.g., *Dancing Dolores devoured a dozen donuts*).

☐ Use alliterative words to create a self-portrait. Then, explain why each word is an appropriate description for an aspect of your life (e.g., *Louis: loud—I like loud music and loud parties*).

☐ Choose one of these alliterative phrases (or write one of your own) as the first line of a short story: *Forgetful Felipe feared . . . , Sad Sue sobbed . . . ,* or *Crazy Christopher crashed . . . .* Use as much alliteration in your story as possible.

☐ Choose one or more of the following verbs (or choose one of your own): *dig, write, yap, boast, careen, act, skip.* Match each verb with an animal or a person that starts with the same sound and create an alliterative sentence (e.g., *The raging rhino ripped the ragged raincoat*).

☐ Create several alliterative want ads to run in your local paper (e.g., *Wanted: Wise worker for window washing*).

☐ Choose one or more of the following adjectives (or choose one of your own): *angry, jealous, slimy, funny, jumpy, zany, outrageous.* Match each adjective with a fruit, vegetable, or household object that starts with the same sound. Add additional words to create an alliterative sentence (e.g., *The bashful banana begged for bagels*).

☐ **Wild Card:** You have been asked to create a time capsule so that people 500 years from now can determine what life was like in your time. What items will you include? Why?

☐ **Free Choice**

Developing Writing Fluency © 2000 Creative Teaching Press

Expressive Writing

15

Author _____ Week Beginning _____

Parallel Paths
Critical Components of Simile and Metaphor

- Compare two ideas using word pictures (e.g., *The frozen pond was a mirror under the skaters' blades*).
- Compare two ideas using the word *like* or *as* (e.g., *The boy was as strong as an ox*).

☐ Create a simile or metaphor that describes a part of your daily life. Use this simile or metaphor as an opening line in a paragraph developing that idea (e.g., *My house is grand central station on the weekend*).

☐ Look around the room you are in. Choose several articles of interest to you. Write a descriptive paragraph describing each object. Use at least one simile or metaphor in each paragraph (e.g., *The teacher's desk is old but sturdy like my Grandpa Joe*).

☐ Compare your life to that of a tree. Use as many similes and metaphors as possible. Consider aspects of the tree such as branches, bark, leaves, and roots.

☐ Pick several of your favorite colors. Create a list of metaphors that express what each color represents to you (e.g., *Red is fire burning hot. Red is a rose opening in the dawn*).

☐ Brainstorm human characteristics and personality traits (e.g., *clever, shy, sly, cowardly*). Think of an animal that could be associated with each characteristic. Write a simile or metaphor for each (e.g., *Janet is clever like a fox*).

☐ Use as many similes and metaphors as possible to create a self-portrait (e.g., *My hair is like newly cut straw. My feelings are tender like a newborn lamb*).

☐ **Wild Card:** Describe several of the simple things in your life that bring you pleasure and delight. Be sure to include favorite objects, sights, and sounds. Tell why these things are special to you.

☐ **Free Choice**

Personality Plus
Critical Component of Personification

- Give human traits to an animal or a nonhuman object (e.g., *The trees shyly peeked through the clouds*).

☐ From the point of view of a newly emerged butterfly, describe a beautiful spring day. Be sure to give the butterfly human emotions, such as happiness, fear, or joy.

☐ Take an imaginary ocean dive in which you see an assortment of exotic, colorful fish. Describe several of these fish and assign them human characteristics based on their behaviors (e.g., *The brilliant angelfish fearfully darted behind the coral reef*).

☐ Develop a conversation between two stately trees that understand they may be cut down. Allow your readers to sense their fear.

☐ Brainstorm as many zoo animals as you can. Give each animal a human characteristic based on its appearance or behavior. Write a short story about the actions of your personified animals.

☐ Picture your favorite setting (e.g., a special beach, a mountain retreat). Brainstorm the elements that are part of this setting. Assign each element a human characteristic (e.g., *mountains: brave and strong, stream: carefree*). Use these personified elements to write a descriptive paragraph (e.g., *The mountains stood brave and tall towering over the carefree stream*).

☐ Brainstorm the items you might find in your refrigerator. Think of an appropriate human characteristic for each item. Write a story about how these personified items might seek to work together to create a special meal (e.g., *The grumpy broccoli finally agreed to be part of the salad*).

☐ **Wild Card:** Describe the clothes people will be wearing 1,000 years from now. Include a rationale, stating why people will need or want to wear each item.

☐ **Free Choice**

Developing Writing Fluency © 2000 Creative Teaching Press

Author _____   Week Beginning _____

Inside Out
Critical Components of Character Emotion

- Use one of the following or a combination of each:
  - external dialogue (e.g., *I had a hard day today*).
  - internal dialogue (e.g., *"I'm never going to make this basket," he thought as he dribbled the ball closer to the hoop*).
  - description (e.g., *She nervously fidgeted with her napkin*).

☐ Brian is usually a calm boy, but today he is very angry because someone stole his bicycle. Without directly stating that Brian is angry, show Brian's anger through what he does and says.

☐ Tiffany is very excited because today is her birthday and she will be having several friends over to celebrate. Show Tiffany's anticipation and excitement through her conversation and actions.

☐ Write about the following: Tyvon is very nervous about going to the doctor because he knows he will need at least two vaccinations. He does not want to admit that he is nervous, but his actions give him away.

☐ Zack is overcome with fear as he looks out his bedroom window and sees a UFO land in his front yard. Soon, two aliens are knocking on his front door. Without stating that Zack is fearful, show your readers his strong emotions.

☐ Think about an activity that you really love and that makes you happy. Develop a scene that shows your enjoyment without directly stating it.

☐ Maria is jealous of her younger sister, Danielle, because she feels that Danielle gets more attention than she does. Create a scene that shows Maria's jealousy through her conversation and actions.

☐ **Wild Card:** You have been given the unusual job of training your huge Saint Bernard dog to help take care of your two-year-old baby sister. What would your training program include and why?

☐ **Free Choice**

Author _____ Week Beginning _____

Show Don't Tell
Critical Components of Strong Verbs

- Show precise action and capture emotion (e.g., *fret, chuckle, announce*).

- Write in the active voice (e.g., *Sam kicked the ball* not *The ball was kicked by Sam*).

☐ Brainstorm as many synonyms as you can for *walk* (e.g., *saunter, jog, limp*). Invent an imaginary character and have him or her take a trip around a city. Use several synonyms for *walked* in your story.

☐ List synonyms for *said* (e.g., *whispered, responded, yelled*). Develop a conversation between three friends who are planning an exciting summer adventure. Avoid using the word *said*.

☐ Think of interesting, active synonyms for *moved* (e.g., *crawled, soared, jettisoned*). Use several of your words to write a story about an alien who has been stranded on Earth and finally returns home.

☐ Brainstorm synonyms for *played* (e.g., *jumped, bicycled, raced*). Use several of your synonyms to write a paragraph about an afternoon of play between James and Michael.

☐ Generate synonyms for *like* (e.g., *enjoy, appreciate*). Write a descriptive paragraph entitled *My Ideal Day*. Use several of your words in your paragraph.

☐ Use as many vivid verbs (e.g., show movement, tell sounds, reveal smells) as possible to describe one or more of the following: a flood, a football game, a parade for an Olympic competition. Be sure to write in the active voice.

☐ **Wild Card:** You and your best friend are lost and must survive on your own for a month. Choose a setting (e.g., New York City, the Alaskan wilderness, the Australian outback, outer space) and tell the story of your adventures.

☐ **Free Choice**

Developing Writing Fluency © 2000 Creative Teaching Press

Mood Mania

Critical Components of Mood

- Include the setting (e.g., *It was a dark and stormy night*).
- Use specific words (e.g., *quaint colonial home* or *cold stony castle*).
- Use words and phrases that heighten the senses and evoke emotion (e.g., *The screeching owl broke the eerie silence*).

☐ Brainstorm words and phrases that create a scary, uncertain mood. Use these phrases to write a paragraph that creates suspense about two children who are lost.

☐ Brainstorm words and phrases that create a serene, peaceful mood. Use these phrases to develop a paragraph that describes a small town on a lazy Sunday afternoon.

☐ Describe a setting that features a circus, sporting event, parade, or any event that creates excitement and a high level of energy.

☐ Describe the ruins of a castle using word choices that create a mood of doom and dread. Then, describe the same castle using word choices that create a mood of romance and nostalgia (desire to return to the past).

☐ Choose one or more of the following subjects: an old farm, a young girl or boy walking down a path, a dense forest. Describe each subject in at least two different ways, using word choices to create varying moods.

☐ Brainstorm the positive and negative aspects of fire. Write one paragraph in which you use fire to create a warm, cozy atmosphere. Write a second paragraph in which fire is used to create a frightening mood.

☐ **Wild Card:** Brainstorm a list of your least favorite foods. Next, write a sentence for each food, stating the nicest thing you can say about it (e.g., *The nicest thing I can say about peas is that they are small and I can swallow them quickly*).

☐ **Free Choice**

Developing Writing Fluency © 2000 Creative Teaching Press

Dear Diary
Critical Components of Journal Writing

- Record events.

- Describe personal feelings, thoughts, and observations.

☐ Author Roald Dahl, who created *James and the Giant Peach,* stated that expressing himself in letters and journals helped him organize his thoughts and increased his fluency as an author. In what one area do you most desire improvement (e.g., basketball skills, playing a musical instrument)? What kind of things can you do to improve your performance? Why is this important to you?

☐ List the things or people that make you feel happy or contented. Explain your answers.

☐ What event in the news concerns you most? Why?

☐ What is it that makes some students so popular? What qualities or characteristics do they have that make others enjoy being with them?

☐ What is your most prized possession? Why is it so important to you?

☐ Leonardo da Vinci, the Italian artist, inventor, and author, kept numerous journals. *I question* were the words most often recorded in his journals. Some of his questions were *I question what would it be like to walk on water? I wonder what causes tickling? Why are the stars invisible during the day?* Brainstorm your own list of questions.

☐ **Wild Card:** Robert Louis Stevenson was inspired to write *Treasure Island* after drawing a treasure map with his stepson, Hyod. If you could design a map of an island on which you would spend a year of your life, what geographical features and natural resources would you want on the island? What kind of house would you live in?

☐ **Free Choice**

Author _____ Week Beginning _____

Sincerely Yours

Critical Components of Friendly Letter Writing

- Begin with a heading (the date).

- Include a greeting (to whom the letter is written), body (the main information in your letter), and closing (a polite good-bye).

- End with a signature (the name of the author).

☐ Write an imaginary thank-you letter, thanking a mysterious benefactor for the gift you would most like to receive.

☐ Write a fictional letter to someone your age who lives in the year 2150. What kind of questions would you like to ask? Tell him or her about your life.

☐ Write a letter to a student who will be in your class next year. Give advice on how to succeed.

☐ Write a letter to your favorite cartoon or comic strip character. Perhaps you can offer a suggestion for a future strip or simply tell why you like the character.

☐ Abraham Lincoln received a great deal of mail during his presidency. He read all his letters and even took the advice of one young girl who suggested that he grow a beard to improve his appearance. Write a letter to the president of the United States or another world leader. What one piece of advice would you give? Why?

☐ Write an imaginary letter to former president John F. Kennedy in which you answer the question he posed in his speech as he was sworn into office: *Ask not what your country can do for you, but ask what you can do for your country.*

☐ **Wild Card:** Create an imaginary planet. This planet is similar to Earth but has several important differences. What is different? Tell how these differences affect the people, what students learn in school, what foods are eaten, what vacations people take, and what jobs and daily tasks are performed.

☐ **Free Choice**

Developing Writing Fluency © 2000 Creative Teaching Press

The Narrative Writing Domain

The narrative domain consists of writing prompts that focus on essential aspects of story, such as setting, character development, and conflict. Additionally, the narrative writing domain has many pages of writing prompts that focus on specific narrative products, such as short stories, tall tales, and fables.

Student Background Knowledge

Some students' parents spent countless hours reading storybooks to them. Some students' storytelling experiences are limited to watching television programs, movies, and videos. Even the rare student with little media or book exposure, has some sense of story, even if it is simply the oral art of storytelling in his or her family. In fact, the oral art of storytelling often-times supercedes the media and is a powerful storytelling heritage! Whatever students bring to their writing, capitalize on these experiences. Get to know your students' experiences with story prior to teaching the narrative domain. Consider starting out your unit on narrative writing by asking students *What is your favorite family story? What is your favorite book? What is your favorite movie?*

It is important in today's diverse society to build a common core of shared stories from which to draw examples. Read aloud a novel such as *Charlotte's Web* by E. B. White. When you discuss character development, relate your main points to Charlotte, Wilbur, or Templeton. Read (novels or picture books) to your students on a regular basis to help build common experiences with setting, character, events, conflict, and resolution. Picture books provide a visual support for the oral vocabulary that is helpful for any age, and especially so for English language learners.

Career Application

Teachers, particularly in the elementary years, tend to overemphasize the narrative domain to the neglect of the other domains. Plan your writing program so that assignments are equally balanced among the four domains. Be sure, however, to emphasize the importance of a story well told, tying in the many career opportunities for those who become skillful in the art of storytelling. For example, novelists, short story authors, scriptwriters, and teachers are but a few of the people whose careers require mastery of storytelling.

Making the Most of the Writing Process

Invite students to bring their favorite books to school. Use these books as springboards for a variety of assignments such as the following:

- Write a sequel to the book.
- Write and illustrate a picture book, telling the same story to a younger child.
- Change the problem in the story. How would the plotline change?
- Retell the story in first or third person.

Most importantly, do not forget the motivation that comes from writing and illustrating original stories to be published and made accessible in your school or classroom library. Students love to read each other's work.

Walkie Talkie

Critical Components of Dialogue

- Record the exact words spoken between two or more characters.
- Begin a new paragraph each time a different person talks.
- Indent paragraphs.
- Use quotation marks to indicate spoken words.
- Keep end punctuation inside quotation marks (e.g., *"Where are you going?"*).
- Use specific verbs to describe spoken words (e.g., *whispered,* not *said*).

☐ Develop the following into an extended dialogue between a cranky adult and an energetic little boy: *"Watch where you're going, young man! You almost knocked me over!"*

☐ Develop a dialogue between an exasperated mother and her five-year-old son. The mother is attempting to entice her son into eating spinach.

☐ Create a dialogue you would like to have with a sports or an entertainment figure.

☐ Develop an imaginary dialogue between you and your pet or an animal you like. What would you say? What might the animal say?

☐ On a quiet September day in 1903, Orville Wright accomplished what no one had done before. He took a twelve-second airplane ride. His brother Wilbur, who had helped design the plane, was eagerly watching and waiting. Create a dialogue you think the brothers might have had after Orville's landing.

☐ Write a dialogue between a towering mountain and a bulldozer that has been hired to gouge a trail through the mountain's center.

☐ **Wild Card:** Describe a pleasant event from a family vacation or outing. Include sensory detail, such as colorful objects and unusual or interesting sounds and textures.

☐ **Free Choice**

Developing Writing Fluency © 2000 Creative Teaching Press

In a Galaxy Far Away
Critical Components of Setting

- Tell where and when the story takes place.

- Use descriptive words and phrases that appeal to the reader's senses (e.g., *In the forest there was little more than green moss, feather-like ferns, and trees towering overhead*).

☐ Develop a setting for a newly discovered planet. When is it discovered? What does it look like? What textures and sounds are present? What unusual features does it have?

☐ Choose one or more of these characters and develop an appropriate setting for them: a knight, a pharaoh, an Indian chief, a lion and her cubs.

☐ Create a story setting for one or more of the following plot ideas: a kidnapping, an angry bear looking for her cubs, a lost motorist.

☐ Create a story setting for one or more of these sports stories: a surfing competition, an Olympic event, a basketball game.

☐ Create the ideal setting for your dream vacation. Where will it be? What will you see, hear, and experience? Be sure to include when your vacation will be.

☐ Include the following items in the setting of a story about an unusual and dangerous camping trip: roaring rapids, overhanging branches, roughly hewn (cut) boulders, and a mountain lion on the prowl for its next meal.

☐ **Wild Card:** You have just returned from outer space. Aliens from another planet abducted you for a three-hour visit to their universe. During these three hours you learned things that will change your life forever. What did you learn?

☐ **Free Choice**

Developing Writing Fluency © 2000 Creative Teaching Press

Author _____   Week Beginning _____

What a Character

Critical Components of Character Development

- Describe the character's appearance, thoughts, and actions.
- Include what other characters say and think about the character.

☐ Develop a paragraph that shows a character who is old physically but acting very childishly.

☐ Write about a character your age who shows one of the following characteristics: generosity, selfishness, anger, dishonesty, or kindness.

☐ Develop a main character for one or more of these story settings: a backpacking trip to the Alps, a remote deserted island, an elementary school office.

☐ Brainstorm a character who has at least two of the following qualities: funny, independent, bright, shy, conceited, inventive, courageous, daring, curious, serious, cooperative, generous. Write a paragraph in which the words and actions of your character demonstrate these characteristics.

☐ When writing *Little Women,* Louisa May Alcott modeled the tomboyish character Jo March after herself. "I am Jo," she often told her friends and family. Invent a character modeled after yourself for a story you would like to write. Describe the character's physical attributes, personality traits, interests, and hobbies.

☐ Picture the following well-used shoes: a worn tennis shoe; an elaborate, newly polished cowboy boot; a high-heeled silver sandal; and a muddy hiking boot. Pick one of these shoes and describe the person who owns this shoe. Include physical attributes as well as personality traits and special interests and activities.

☐ **Wild Card:** Imagine you are 70 years old. What has your life been like since you were the age you are now? Did you get married and have a family? What jobs did you have? Where did you travel and vacation?

☐ **Free Choice**

Developing Writing Fluency © 2000 Creative Teaching Press

Conflicting Forces
Critical Components of Conflict

- Describe the central problem the main character(s) faces.

- Have the problem fall into one of three categories: character against character, character against him/herself, character against nature.

☐ Mark Twain's plot for *Tom Sawyer* was prompted by a newspaper story about caves that Twain had explored as a boy. Develop a recent news event into a short story. Who are the characters? What is a possible conflict and resolution?

☐ Brainstorm a conflict between a character and nature. Perhaps your character is battling the elements in a wild winter storm or a raging ocean or is stranded on a deserted island.

☐ Brainstorm a conflict between a character and his or her own fears and emotions (e.g., fear and self-doubt related to an upcoming challenge, grief and loss due to death or divorce).

☐ At one time in his life, Jack London, who wrote *The Call of the Wild,* was arrested for being a vagrant and sent to jail without an opportunity for a fair trial. London's feelings of being unjustly treated surfaced in many of his writings. Think back to a time when you or someone you know was unjustly treated. Use this situation to create a conflict for a story plot.

☐ Vincent van Gogh, the Dutch painter famous for impassioned paintings such as *Starry Night* and *Sunflowers,* never achieved recognition in his lifetime. In fact, people often reacted to him with either laughter or fear. Develop a conflict about a gifted but unusual character and his or her judgmental neighbors.

☐ Gertrude Ederte was the first woman to swim across the icy English Channel. She battled more than 20 miles of cold, choppy water; high winds; powerful currents; and the stings of jellyfish. Write a story highlighting her conflict with nature.

☐ **Wild Card:** Tell as much as you can about yourself by creating a name poem. Create more poems for your friends or family. For example:
Sometimes silly
Always on the move
Music lover extraordinaire

☐ **Free Choice**

Developing Writing Fluency © 2000 Creative Teaching Press

My Point of View
Critical Components of First Person Point of View

- Tell the story from the perspective of a main character (e.g., *I went down the street to visit my sister Sara*).

- Use pronouns like *I, me, my, our,* and *us.*

- Provide limited knowledge—the reader can only know what happens through the main character's experience. Thoughts and opinions of the rest of the characters can only be surmised through the mind of the main character.

- Reveal the main character's thoughts, feelings, and ideas.

☐ From the first person perspective, create an adventure in a hot-air balloon. Where would you go? What would you take with you? Would you travel alone or with someone else? What dangers would you encounter?

☐ From the perspective of a cunning and hungry hammerhead shark, create a story about two teenagers who have been caught in a storm and are now lost at sea in a small sailboat. A deserted island is nearby if only they can reach it.

☐ From the first person perspective, create a story incorporating the following items: a full moon, approaching footsteps, an abandoned cabin, and a broken ham radio.

☐ You are a faithful golden retriever named Bones, owned by a twelve-year-old. From your perspective, relate the story of how you woke up one night to find yourself in a haze of thick smoke and shattered glass. What do you do?

☐ From a first person perspective, write a story that either describes a horrendous day or a magnificent day.

☐ Jesse Owens, the legendary African American track star, won four gold medals at the 1936 Olympic games where Adolf Hitler was seeking to use the games to support his theory of white supremacy. Jesse was quoted as saying, "It was a million thrills packed into one." Write Jesse's story from a first person perspective. You may choose to be Jesse himself, an Olympic official, or a fan in the audience.

☐ **Wild Card:** If you could be on any television show, which one would you pick? What part would you play? Why would you want to play this part?

☐ **Free Choice**

Author _____ Week Beginning _____

Their Point of View
Critical Components of Third Person Point of View

- Tell the story from the perspective of a narrator (e.g., *Donna went down the street to visit her friend Sara*).

- Use pronouns like *he, she, it, they, him,* and *her*.

- Consider using an omniscient narrator who sees everyone and knows everything.

☐ Anne Frank's original journals included daydreams, thoughts on numerous subjects, and various short stories. She sometimes used her personal experiences as a springboard to fiction writing, distancing herself from her experiences through the use of a third person narrator. Brainstorm an interesting or a difficult experience you have had. Use this as a basis for a fiction story told in the third person.

☐ Brainstorm some of the problems you, your friends, or family members have experienced (e.g., ran out of gas, gotten lost, flunked a test). Create a short story depicting one of these problems. Tell your story from a third person perspective.

☐ You are walking by yourself along a lonely stretch of beach. You look down and spot an old, rusted set of keys. From a third person perspective, write a story about these mysterious keys. To whom do they belong? What secrets will they unlock?

☐ Think of a special event that has recently happened in your school or neighborhood, such as a parade or basketball game. Next, brainstorm possible problems or conflicts that could have occurred at the event. From a third person perspective, describe the event, the conflict, and a possible resolution.

☐ From a third person perspective, write a story about an abandoned dog named Loner. How did he get his name? How does he survive? What problems does he encounter?

☐ J.R.R. Tolkien, author of *The Hobbit,* wrote about unusual heroes. He believed that a hero, no matter how small or insignificant, could triumph over the world's evils. Create your own unusual hero. What makes your hero unusual? What conflict does he or she experience? How does your hero triumph over this conflict? Tell your hero's story from a third person perspective.

☐ **Wild Card:** Fredric Chopin was a Polish composer of expressive music. He loved his country deeply. When he left Poland at the age of 20, he took with him a cup of Polish dirt. If you were forced to leave your country, what things would you take to remind yourself of your roots and heritage?

☐ **Free Choice**

Author _____ Week Beginning _____

And to Think It Happened to Me

Critical Components of Autobiographical Incidents

- Describe a single event in your life.
- Write in the first person.
- Describe the details about the event in sequential order.

☐ Think back to your first year in school and describe one event. Be sure to tell about the setting, including where you went to school and how the others involved were related to you (e.g., your teacher, your close friend).

☐ Write about a time when something unusual or interesting happened when you were baby-sitting or when a baby-sitter was in charge of you.

☐ Write about an experience you had with a grandparent or an older person. What did you learn?

☐ Red Grange is the electrifying football player who is credited with popularizing this sport. In high school he delivered blocks of ice weighing 200 pounds. He said he did this to keep himself " tough as nails." Write about the most difficult physical challenge you ever experienced.

☐ We all enjoy looking back on special times in our lives. Choose one or more of the following and take a trip down memory lane: *The bravest thing I ever did was _____, The most embarrassing thing I ever did was _____, or The most fun I ever had was _____.*

☐ Describe a favorite birthday celebration. What did you do to celebrate? Whom were you with? What made the celebration so special?

☐ **Wild Card:** Discuss the dos and don'ts of being a good friend. Entitle your essay *The Ten Rules of Friendship.*

☐ **Free Choice**

Developing Writing Fluency © 2000 Creative Teaching Press

Author _____ Week Beginning _____

Tell Me a Story
Critical Components of Short Stories

- Include a strong beginning that grabs the reader's attention, establishes the setting, and introduces the characters.

- Add events that lead to a conflict.

- Finish with a conclusion that usually resolves the conflict.

☐ Create a short story that incorporates the following elements: a time machine, a broken dial, a secret tunnel, and a dark dungeon.

☐ Author Ray Bradbury, who wrote *The Martian Chronicles,* often got ideas for his stories by brainstorming lists of words—things that were associated with each other. Brainstorm your own set of words. Start with one word and then include people, places, events, and emotions related to your first word. Use this list to spark a short story idea.

☐ Complete the following sentence to create an unusual conflict and resolution: *Everyone was waiting for me to open that last gift, but no one was prepared for ....*

☐ Create a beginning and middle for one of the following story endings:
  - *They turned, smiled sadly, tiptoed silently down the path, and were never heard from again.*
  - *And that was how Grandpa earned the nickname Wild Will.*
  - *"See how brave my daughter is? I knew she could handle the situation," the woman proudly stated.*

☐ In *The Borrowers,* Mary Norton wrote a story about very little people and their exciting, humorous adventures. Imagine little people who live in your house. What would they look like? Where would they live? What problems would they encounter? Create a short story based on their adventures.

☐ Develop a short story that has a mood of uncertainty and creates the emotions of fear and worry. Your two main characters are two teenagers who have become stranded on a backpacking trip. Describe the setting and develop events that lead to their conflict. How is the conflict resolved?

☐ **Wild Card:** Bruce Lee greatly influenced the growth of the martial arts in the United States. The words used most to describe him were intense, impatient, and strong (he could do one-finger push-ups). What three words would people use to describe you? Why?

☐ **Free Choice**

Developing Writing Fluency © 2000 Creative Teaching Press

Narrative Writing

Author _____ Week Beginning _____

On a Dark and Stormy Night

Critical Components of Mystery/Suspense

- Include an introduction, a problem, and a resolution.

- Explore and solve a mysterious situation (e.g., a disappearance, a death, an unusual occurrence).

- Use language that captures the emotion of the events as the story unfolds (e.g., communicates feelings of anxiety, uncertainty, and worry).

☐ What if? You're walking along a deserted beach when suddenly out of nowhere a set of footprints appears. Where did they come from? Where are they going?

☐ Develop this mystery idea: You are alone watching a young child in a large old house in a lonely neighborhood. It is getting rather late and suddenly you hear someone or something at the window. What happens next?

☐ Develop a mystery about lost treasure entitled *The Buried Treasure Mystery*. Include details about the legend behind the treasure. Where is it hidden? Who is searching for it and why?

☐ Use this opening to write a story: *I awoke with a start. It was pitch black and I couldn't see a thing, but I felt a presence, a strange unearthly presence.*

☐ Develop a story about a mysterious stranger who suddenly appears in your neighborhood. Who is this stranger? What is his or her secret? As you write, build suspense. Give your story a mysterious mood.

☐ Develop this story idea: One night you are quietly watching television when suddenly the lights flicker and a strange man comes on the screen and begins talking directly to you. He knows your name and knows you are home alone.

☐ **Wild Card:** You are a freshly picked South American banana. Describe your life from the time you were plucked off the tree to your demise.

☐ **Free Choice**

Author _____ Week Beginning _____

Pages of History
Critical Components of Historical Fiction

- Include an introduction, a problem, and a resolution.

- Set the story in a specific place and time period (e.g., colonial America, ancient Greece).

- Provide accurate information about the life and general events of the people in this place and time period.

- Weave in fictional aspects (e.g., a fictional character, elaboration on an historical event about which there is no historical record).

☐ Ester Forbes created a historical world in her novel *Johnny Tremain*. Johnny, a teenage boy, meets historical characters such as Paul Revere and John Hancock and witnesses the Boston Tea Party. Which historical event would you most like to witness? Develop a short story centered on this event.

☐ Take a trip back in time and write a short story about one of the following: a rider making a first-time delivery for the Pony Express or Neil Armstrong taking the first step on the Moon.

☐ Rembrant is considered to be the greatest master of the Dutch School of Art. He painted many elaborate historical scenes as well as expressive portraits of himself and others. If you were a master painter and were asked to portray two important historical events, what events would you choose and why? Brainstorm the characters and conflict that would be present in your painting.

☐ Pretend you are standing at the door of a time machine. The panel to your right has a series of numbers. Push in a date and request a destination. In an instant you will arrive there. Assume the identity of one of the characters in your historical destination and write about his or her adventure.

☐ Write a short story for one of the following titles: *The Knight's Best Memory, The Day Old Jake Finally Struck It Rich*, or *The Wright Brothers' Bumpy Ride*.

☐ Write a story about a servant girl or boy who lives in one of the following places: an Egyptian palace, a Chinese palace, or an English castle.

☐ **Wild Card:** Brainstorm all the words that come to your mind when you think of the word *water* (e.g., *swimming, salty, sprinkling, drinking*). Next, describe your thoughts about water or write about your favorite "water" experience.

☐ **Free Choice**

Developing Writing Fluency © 2000 Creative Teaching Press

Author _____ Week Beginning _____

Telling Tales
Critical Components of Tall Tales

- Create a short story that introduces a larger-than-life character.
- Include exaggeration.
- Include a problem and a resolution that involves the special skills and abilities of the main character.

☐ Write a tall tale that exaggerates your abilities or an accomplishment you recently completed.

☐ Include one of your friends or family members in a tall tale, focusing on one of his or her accomplishments. Be sure to include a title that captures the person's skill.

☐ Choose one of the following characters: Doc Dani, Long-Nosed Larry, Detective Deb, or Mountain Man Mike. Make up an amazing feat accomplished as a result of the character's skill in a particular area. Write a paragraph describing this feat.

☐ Babe Ruth is considered the best player in American baseball history. He is most famous for hitting more than 700 home runs. Create a tall tale about Babe, exaggerating his tremendous baseball abilities.

☐ Mia Hamm, the American women's soccer superstar, is one of the most popular players of the most popular sport in the world. Write a tall tale about Mia and her amazing abilities.

☐ Johnny Weissmuller was a record-breaking American swimmer and winner of five gold medals at the 1924 and 1928 Olympics. He later became famous as Tarzan because he played the hero in 19 Tarzan movies. Write a tall tale about Tarzan's amazing jungle feats.

☐ **Wild Card:** Pretend you are a gifted painter. Everything you paint is destined to become a masterpiece. What would you choose to paint? Explain your answer.

☐ **Free Choice**

Author _____ Week Beginning _____

Once upon a Time
Critical Components of Fairy Tales

- Involve love and/or adventure (e.g., the story of Snow White).
- Include a fairy-tale opening (e.g., *Once upon a time* or *Long ago when wishes still came true*).
- Include a magical event or magical powers as a key element in the story.
- Feature a hero or heroine and a villain.
- End happily ever after.

☐ Create a fairy tale set in an enchanted forest. Your characters can include a talking forest, a magical rock, and a sly old elf who controls the forest's strange powers.

☐ Develop a fairy tale in which you are the hero or heroine. Where and when will the tale take place? What magical powers will you possess? What evil force will you conquer?

☐ Think of your favorite fairy tale. Maybe it is Snow White, Cinderella, Hansel and Gretel, or the Princess and the Pea. Retell this tale from the perspective of the villain.

☐ Complete this tale: Long ago when wishes still came true, there lived a beautiful princess who enchanted all who saw her. The king adored her and granted her every wish, but still the princess grew sadder with each passing day.

☐ Hans Christian Andersen was the Danish author who wrote many famous fairy tales, including *Thumbelina* and *The Little Mermaid*. He had a difficult life and once told his mother, "First one has to endure terrible adversity, then you become famous." Create a fairy tale that features a hero or heroine who triumphs after adversity, becomes famous, and lives happily ever after.

☐ Complete this story about Edwin's latest adventure serving his king: Edwin was a knight full of honor and valor. He was loyal to his king and served him faithfully, without fear. Yet even Edwin's large, strong hands shook as he read the king's latest orders.

☐ **Wild Card:** Leonardo da Vinci, the famous Italian painter and sculptor, loved to play practical jokes. Once he frightened a group of friends by unleashing what appeared to be a dragon but was actually a large but harmless lizard. What is the most outlandish practical joke that has ever happened to you or a friend?

☐ **Free Choice**

Developing Writing Fluency © 2000 Creative Teaching Press

The Tortoise and the Hare

Critical Components of Fables

- Create a fanciful tale that includes animal characters that talk and act like people.
- Introduce a problem related to the weakness of a character who ultimately learns a lesson.
- Include an introduction, a problem, and a resolution.
- End with a moral or lesson that summarizes the fable.

☐ Choose several animals that most amuse you. Pick a human characteristic to represent each one. Develop a fable about two of these animals.

☐ Pick animals to represent you and a friend. Next, pick human characteristics to represent each of you. Create a fable in which you or your friend learn(s) an important lesson.

☐ Write a fable that concludes with one of the following morals: "Pride goeth before a fall," "Don't count your chickens before they're hatched," or "Look before you leap."

☐ Write a fable entitled *The Ostrich Who Wanted to Fly*. Perhaps your moral could be, "Be happy with your own talents and abilities."

☐ In *The Ant and the Grasshopper*, the moral is "Prepare today for tomorrow's needs." In the original story, the ant prepares while the grasshopper sings and plays. Rewrite the story, casting the grasshopper as the wise insect who prepares for the future.

☐ Fables use human weaknesses to teach a lesson. If you were an invisible person and could see and hear everything going on around you, which of the following human weaknesses would you use in a fable: greed, cowardice, unkindness, indifference, dishonesty? Explain your answer.

☐ **Wild Card:** Ludwig van Beethoven was a prolific composer who wrote nine symphonies. He worked best at night. Often after working all night long, he poured ice cold water over his head to keep awake. When are you the most productive? What do you do to motivate yourself? How do you keep going when you want to quit?

☐ **Free Choice**

The Informative Writing Domain

The informative domain consists of foundational concepts, such as writing strong thesis statements and paragraphs. The majority of the writing prompts in this domain, however, consist of informative products, such as how-tos, biographical sketches, news articles, and scientific writing.

Student Background Knowledge

The informative domain taps into the interests of those students who are perhaps less creative and more serious about their writing content. In other words, some students would prefer to write a report on outer space than to create an imaginary story. To tap into interests of both types of students, use the prompts in this section that can be both fact oriented and creative.

Career Application

Time spent in the informative domain prepares students to think in an organized fashion about their writing. Having students focus on a particular aspect of informative writing, such as writing a thesis statement, is helpful practice for learning how to succinctly organize thoughts. This is helpful in any career where writing reports is a frequent requirement (e.g., accounting, sales).

Making the Most of the Writing Process

In an effort to bring joy and creativity into the writing process, it is important for you to write along with the students (just as you would during SSR) and to allow students to share their writing on a regular basis. Humorous pieces often emerge during CDW as students spontaneously let their thoughts flow. Read aloud your writing to students. Students find this fascinating and learn from you as you share reflective thoughts on your own writing.

In a Nutshell
Critical Components of Thesis Statements

- Include a thesis statement that drives the organization of an informative piece.

- Be concise. Avoid unnecessary words and description.

- Include at least three main points about a topic (e.g., *To be an effective basketball player one needs to know the basic rules of the game, strategies for improving your performance, and how to work as part of a team*).

☐ Write a thesis statement that describes three main points about a favorite sport or hobby. Then, write as much as you know about each point.

☐ Choose your favorite book or movie. Write a thesis statement that describes the three most important reasons why you like the story. Elaborate on each point.

☐ Think about something you have always wanted to do, but have not done yet. For example, maybe you want to scuba dive, parachute, travel to Paris, live in a mansion, buy a German shepherd, or catch a shark. Write a thesis statement describing the three most important reasons why you want to do this. Then, tell your readers about these three reasons in detail.

☐ Some students hate school. Some students like school. Write a thesis statement describing how you feel about school. Include three reasons for why you feel this way. Then, write a paragraph, elaborating on each point. Be as specific as possible.

☐ Every once in awhile, something really embarrassing happens. For example, one time a girl's piano music blew away during a recital and she tripped as she walked off the stage. A student got salad stuck on his braces and smiled all day without knowing it. What was your most embarrassing moment? Write a thesis statement, telling your readers three main reasons for your being embarrassed. Elaborate on each main point and why it was so awful!

☐ Someone tempts you to take drugs. Write a thesis statement describing three main reasons why you will say NO! Elaborate on those points.

☐ **Wild Card:** Imagine yourself at the beach, in the desert, or in the mountains. List everything you know about this environment.

☐ **Free Choice**

Building Blocks
Critical Components of Paragraph Writing

- Write a topic sentence that informs the reader what the paragraph is about (e.g., *Dogs are friendly creatures*).

- Include at least two to four supporting sentences that give more detail (e.g., *Dogs like to romp and play. Dogs often wag their tails when they meet someone new. Dogs enjoy chasing balls*).

☐ Write a paragraph about a member of your family. In the topic sentence, tell one thing that is special about the person. Write supporting sentences that elaborate on this character. Write additional paragraphs about other family members.

☐ Positive character qualities, like kindness, responsibility, and respect, are very important. Choose a character quality that you possess. Write a topic sentence about it. Add additional detail with supporting sentences. Consider several other positive qualities you possess and write paragraphs about these also.

☐ Are you hungry right now? Ready for lunch or a good snack? Write a paragraph about what a person should eat for breakfast, lunch, or dinner. In the topic sentence, be sure to tell which meal you will describe. In supporting sentences, tell about the common types of food choices that are healthy and delicious.

☐ Have you traveled to an interesting place for vacation or on a drive with your family? Or, have you visited a friend's house or apartment that you found interesting? If so, write a paragraph about that place. Name the place in your topic sentence and add supporting sentences that provide detail. Write additional paragraphs about other places you have visited and enjoyed.

☐ What animal do you know the most about? Write a topic sentence about this animal. Add more detail in supporting sentences. Write one or more paragraphs about this animal, sharing your expertise.

☐ What do you like to do for a hobby? Play ball? Ride bikes? Play games? Write a paragraph about your hobby. Write other paragraphs that describe other favorite activities.

☐ **Wild Card:** Write a letter to the president. State your opinion on subjects that are important to you, such as war, ecology, and education.

☐ **Free Choice**

Opposites Attract
Critical Components of Compare/Contrast

- Use precise word choice.

- Compare two things or ideas (i.e., tell how the things or ideas are similar).

- Contrast the two things or ideas (i.e., tell point-by-point differences).

- Use comparison words and phrases (e.g., *compared to, however, but, whereas, similarly*).

☐ Think about two people you know who are very different. Compare and contrast their personalities and preferences (e.g., what they like and don't like).

☐ Choose two geographical environments (e.g., desert, mountain, forest, plains, tundra). Compare and contrast these two types of environments (e.g., *Both the plains and tundra tend to be flat; however, the tundra is a much colder climate*).

☐ Rachel Carson, a respected ecologist, wrote a book called *Silent Spring*. When you read her title, you automatically compare and contrast what you know about spring (e.g., noisy with the sounds of birds and people outdoors) with the scene her title describes. Her title is meant to hook the reader and get him or her to pick up the book to read more about what she believed to be happening in the environment. Brainstorm a list of short phrases that imply a comparison or contrast and then briefly explain how each of your phrases does so.

☐ Do you or someone you know speak two different languages? Describe how the languages are the same or different. For example, Spanish and English have many similar words. In English we would say, *The banana is delicious.* Similarly, in Spanish we would say, *La banana esta deliciosa.*

☐ Compare and contrast an academic subject that you love with one that you hate.

☐ Compare and contrast the difference between reading a book and watching a movie.

☐ **Wild Card:** Record everything you know about the sun. Write a descriptive paragraph in which the sun is beneficial and one in which the sun is harmful.

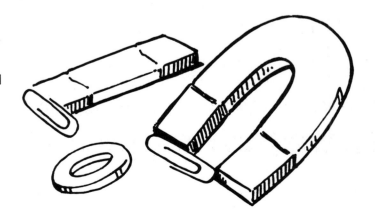

☐ **Free Choice**

Author _____ Week Beginning _____

Problem Solvers
Critical Components of Problem/Solution

- Include a clear explanation of the problem (e.g., *Dogs are getting lost*).

- Suggest possible solutions to the problem (e.g., *Require collars and tags. Add identification codes to dogs' teeth. All dogs must be on a leash or behind a fence*).

- Identify actual solution(s) to the problem, if one(s) exists.

☐ Describe a problem you are having at school and discuss several possible solutions.

☐ Describe a problem you are having at home and discuss several possible solutions.

☐ Consider how you might cheer up a friend who is feeling blue. Describe possible ways to lift your friend from the doldrums.

☐ Think about something that is a "pain" to you. For example, maybe your backpack is too heavy, you always forget your lunch, or your shoelaces wear out. Think up several possible solutions or inventions that might solve this problem. Describe these possibilities to your readers.

☐ Brainstorm a list of ways you could earn money for an upcoming school activity or family vacation. Choose one that appeals to you and describe exactly how it could be accomplished, including who else might be involved and what each person's role would be.

☐ Imagine that you will be living on a space station for two full years. What types of problems might you encounter and what are some possible solutions to these problems?

☐ **Wild Card:** In some cultures, children are given names that reflect their character. If you could choose any name for yourself, what would it be? Why do you think this is an ideal name for you?

☐ **Free Choice**

Developing Writing Fluency © 2000 Creative Teaching Press

Author _____ Week Beginning _____

In the news
Critical Components of News Bites

- Write concise updates on news events.
- Use approximately 60–120 words.
- Answer the questions who, what, where, when, why, and how.

☐ Fourth of July is a favorite American holiday. Pretend that you have just met someone from another country who has never heard of the Fourth of July. Describe the origin, traditions, foods, and activities common to this holiday.

☐ Someone has just done something very kind for your friend. You will be the reporter on tonight's news. Write a short news bite, describing what happened. Be sure to include who, what, when, where, why, and how!

☐ What was the most important event that ever happened to you? Perhaps it was the day you met your best friend, the day of your First Communion, the day your family adopted your sister, or the day your dog had puppies. Write a news bite, concisely describing who, what, where, when, why, and how this happened.

☐ One evening, you and your friends were playing, when all of a sudden there was a bright light and an unusual humming noise. Flying towards you was a UFO. Scared speechless, you took in this unusual scene. Write a news bite that concisely describes your experience for tonight's news.

☐ You are in Ülm, Germany, and have just climbed hundreds of stairs to the top of the tallest church in the world, Ülm Cathedral. Gargoyles (ugly decorative figures) surround you. Birds fly around you. You are dizzy with the height and delight, overwhelmed by beauty as you overlook the city. You are asked to report your experience for tonight's news. Write a short news bite, sharing your exhilarating experience.

☐ Many of us have experienced natural disasters. Use your experience to tell about the most horrendous tornado, flood, lightning storm, or earthquake. Write a news bite for tonight's news.

☐ **Wild Card:** Choose one of the following letters: *b, c, d, f, k, m, r, s,* or *t.* Write as many words that start with that letter as possible. Use some of these words in an alliterative sentence or poem. For example, *Delightful Debbie devoured a dozen dunking donuts.*

☐ **Free Choice**

Developing Writing Fluency © 2000 Creative Teaching Press

Author _____ Week Beginning _____

Read All about It

Critical Components of News Articles

- Include a byline, indicating the author's name.

- Answer the questions who, what, where, when, why, and how.

- Begin with key information in the first paragraph, followed by less important details.

☐ In 1860, the Pony Express was established between Missouri and California. Mostly teenagers were chosen as riders. Pay was good, but riding was risky. Imagine that you are a rider who weathered the worst snowstorm imaginable and then was attacked by bandits. Write your news article for the local paper.

☐ You entered your pumpkin in the county fair and won first prize for the finest, largest pumpkin in your county. Write a news article detailing the event.

☐ Pretend it is December 10, 1848, and you have just struck gold in Northern California. Write a news article for your local paper back home. Be sure to tell everyone the full story of who, what, where, when, why, and how.

☐ You have just saved your little brother's life. What happened? Write a news article detailing the events and the accolades you received.

☐ Harriet Ross Tubman was born into slavery in Maryland. She was raised under harsh conditions. At the age of 12 she was seriously injured by a blow to the head for refusing to help tie up a man who had tried to escape. At the age of 30 she escaped from slavery and later returned to Maryland to rescue others. She is believed to have conducted approximately 300 persons to freedom. You are assisting Harriet Tubman in the 1800s with the Underground Railroad. Finally, the Civil War is over and the slaves are free. Write a news article for a northern paper describing your experiences.

☐ It is 1926. Traveling through France, you have just seen for the first time Claude Monet's painting *Waterlilies*. Write an article describing Monet, the art show of his incredible masterpieces at his estate gardens in Giverney, and how the crowd responded.

☐ **Wild Card:** Use words to paint a picture of the messiest room you can imagine (e.g., *I open the door to a wild avalanche of crusty clothing, the smell of old gym socks, and a floor of moldy pizza and sticky soda cans*).

☐ **Free Choice**

NEWS HOUND
PRESIDENT GETS NEW DOG
WASHINGTON D.C.

In Your Dreams...

Critical Components of Brochures

- Provide factual information about a specific place or product.
- Present information in a concise format.
- Include maps, graphics, and/or photographs to enhance the written information.

☐ Think back to the most wonderful place you ever visited on a family vacation or field trip. Perhaps it was Yosemite National Park, New York City, a museum, or the desert. Write brochure text for this location.

☐ Imagine an amusement park that exceeds the hopes of any child. Think about the park and its themes, rides, stores, restaurants, and any other unique amusement activities. Write brochure text highlighting the significant features of the park.

☐ Consider all the most pertinent facts and positive features about the school you currently attend. If you were a new student, what types of information would you like to know on your first day of school? Write the text for a brochure for your school.

☐ One day humankind may have space colonies. Imagine where a space colony might be and how it might be designed. Write the text for a brochure to inform U.S. citizens about how they can apply to live in the space colony for two years.

☐ Imagine you own a game store. Oftentimes adults want to purchase gifts for their children, but they ask, "What types of games would my twelve-year-old enjoy?" You decide to design brochures that have the answers. Choose an age (e.g., nine-year-olds, thirteen-year-olds). Write brochure text that tells the parents everything they need to know about this age to make a wise gift choice.

☐ Write a brochure that describes your favorite car, restaurant, house, or store.

☐ **Wild Card:** Grace Hopper was the "mother" of modern computers. The Navy and the computer industry considered her so valuable that they kept returning her to active duty after she retired. In addition to the computers and computer languages she invented, she coined the term "computer bug" after finding a moth had caused her computer to "crash." If you could ask her several questions, what would you ask and why?

☐ **Free Choice**

Raucous Recipes

Critical Components of Recipes

- Include a title.
- Tell each ingredient.
- Give precise measurements.
- Write step-by-step directions.

☐ Write out a recipe for your favorite main dish. Include the oven temperature and how long you should cook this dish.

☐ Write out a recipe for your favorite dessert, real or imaginary. Be sure to include a creative name and step-by-step directions.

☐ Create a recipe for taking care of your favorite pet, real or imaginary. Ingredients might include a daily dose of hugs, grooming, delicious meals and treats, and some interesting anecdotes.

☐ Create a recipe for finding and keeping a best friend. Be sure to include directions for how to treat this person so he or she will be a lifelong friend.

☐ Choose something that you do well (e.g., art, photography, baseball, singing). If you draw well, write out a recipe for the novice who wants to be good at drawing. Or, if you know how to play the piano, write out a recipe for getting started.

☐ Sometimes it is difficult to be a big brother or sister or a little brother or sister. Sometimes it is difficult to be a good neighbor. Write out a recipe for success in one of these areas.

☐ **Wild Card:** You have been asked to design a new land for Disneyland. What theme would you choose? What rides, activities, and special souvenirs would be available?

☐ **Free Choice**

Developing Writing Fluency © 2000 Creative Teaching Press

Author _____ Week Beginning _____

Compass Rose
Critical Components of Directions

- Be short and concise.
- Use directional words and phrases (e.g., *north, south, east, west, left, right, straight ahead*).
- Include precise numbers, accurate street names, and landmarks.

☐ You have an eighteen-year-old foreign exchange student coming to live with you, and he will have a car. Write precise directions from your house to school and other important places. Include street names, approximate distances, directional words, and important landmarks.

☐ It is the 1800s and you live in Independence, Missouri. You have decided to take your family west. Your cousin is coming from the East Coast, and he will be several days behind you in travel. Send your cousin directions, including the name of the trail(s) you will take (e.g., Santa Fe, Oregon, and/or California Trails), states you will travel through, landmarks, and so forth. Be as precise as possible. Your cousin is traveling alone.

☐ William Clark and Meriwether Lewis were commissioned by President Thomas Jefferson to explore lands acquired through the Louisiana Purchase. A Shoshone guide, Sacajawea, accompanied them and saved their lives several times. In the role of Clark, Lewis, or Sacajawea, describe the most beautiful sight you found along the Missouri, Yellowstone, or Columbia River. Provide directions for others to come to enjoy the sights.

☐ A new student is joining your class and she is deaf. She reads and writes English very well. Help her out. Prepare directions for how to buy lunch, what to do if she gets sick, how to find the restroom, how to check out books, and how to get to the office.

☐ In 1521 Ferdinand Magellan became the first sailor to circumnavigate the globe. Decide on a starting-point and write directions needed by a sailor to sail around the world!

☐ People who deliver letters for the post office are very busy. A new person applies for the job and asks you for advice. Write directions to help familiarize him or her with your neighborhood. Provide tips on the most efficient route to deliver the mail.

☐ **Wild Card:** Use the following nouns (or choose your own) in alliterative sentences: *automobile, emergency, ship, parachute, trap* (e.g., *clubhouse: Crazy cubs convene at the corner clubhouse*).

☐ **Free Choice**

Heroes and Heroines
Critical Components of Biographical Sketches

- Include information about the person's life in chronological order.
- Provide basic factual information (e.g., birthplace, dates of important events).
- Include a few brief, interesting anecdotes.

☐ Choose a famous hero or heroine that you have studied, such as a president, a sports figure, a musician, an artist, or an author. Write a biographical sketch, depicting his or her life for someone who is meeting this person for the first time.

☐ Who is your favorite family member, past or present? Write a biographical sketch about his or her life. Be thorough and accurate—your parents want to keep your sketch in the family album.

☐ Imagine that you are about to write your pen pal for the very first time. Write a biographical sketch about your own life. Be sure to include pertinent facts, such as date of birth and birthplace, places you have lived, and schools you have attended.

☐ Write a biographical sketch about your sister or brother.

☐ Charlotte and Wilbur were interesting characters in E. B. White's *Charlotte's Web*. Write a biographical sketch of one of their lives or any other famous animal character.

☐ Choose a character from your favorite movie or television show. Write a character sketch for him or her.

☐ **Wild Card:** Emily Dickinson is one of America's most beloved poets. Her poems are known for their unique first lines, such as, "I'm nobody! Who are you?" Brainstorm unusual first lines for several original poems.

☐ **Free Choice**

Developing Writing Fluency © 2000 Creative Teaching Press

Tool Time
Critical Components of How-tos

- Begin with a title (e.g., *How to Build a Birdhouse, How to Mow the Lawn, How to Grow Tomatoes*).
- Give step-by-step instructions.
- Use concise words and phrases.
- Include directional words (e.g., *left, right, up, down*).
- Provide exact numbers (e.g., amounts, measurements, time, temperature, miles).

☐ Describe how to build something, such as a birdhouse, a clubhouse, a model car, or a dollhouse.

☐ Describe how to fix something, like a flat tire, a broken friendship, or a messy room.

☐ Write out in detail how to do something in school. For example, how does a person learn to do long division, write a report, or become a member of a basketball team?

☐ Imagine an alien has just landed on planet Earth. He has never been to a sporting goods store, a clothing store, a school, a library, or a restaurant. The alien is very nervous, but anxious to learn. Choose one of the locations and write step-by-step directions on what to do, how to behave, and what to say to people. Be sure to tell about important concepts (e.g., if you are describing a grocery store, the alien needs to know about money, aisles, produce, the frozen food section).

☐ Think about your future goals. Maybe you want to become a professional athlete, an astronaut, a movie star, or a musician. Describe step-by-step the process it will take to get there.

☐ Consider what it takes to be an excellent president. In your own words, write a "how-to" for anyone who might want to become the president. Think about what jobs they should do before they become president, what kinds of experiences they should have, and what kinds of personal character qualities they will need to develop to be successful.

☐ **Wild Card:** Record everything you know about energy (e.g., sources of energy, kinds of energy, positive and negative uses of energy). Describe why you think it is important to conserve energy and give your readers a few ways to do so.

☐ **Free Choice**

Developing Writing Fluency © 2000 Creative Teaching Press

Author _____ Week Beginning _____

Time Travel
Critical Components of Historical Writing

- Tell the events in chronological order.
- Describe the setting, historical figures, and major events.
- Include important smaller facts and details.

☐ Who is your favorite musician from the past (e.g., Mozart), author (e.g., C. S. Lewis), artist (e.g., Monet), or athlete (e.g., Martina Navratilova)? Write a chronological account about his or her life.

☐ Think about your parents, grandparents, and great grandparents. Were they immigrants? Did they move from one state to another? Tell your family history and how you came to live in your current location.

☐ Describe important events that led to the forming of the United States of America.

☐ Think about your favorite historical character. Perhaps it is Sojourner Truth, Abraham Lincoln, Martin Luther King Jr., Sacajawea, or Abigail Adams. Tell the story of his or her life and why he or she is an important historical character.

☐ Imagine it is 60 years from now and you have lived a wonderful life, accomplishing many excellent things to help your community. Write about your life, highlighting your accomplishments and why you will go down in the pages of history.

☐ Think about someone you know who has accomplished many excellent things in his or her life. Perhaps your mother has run an important business and employed a lot of people in your community. Perhaps your spiritual leader (e.g., minister, priest, rabbi) has helped many people in crisis, even writing books on the subject. Perhaps your uncle is raising great kids, is good to his family, and helps his neighbors and community at home and in business. Identify this person and chronologically describe the important contributions of his or her life.

☐ **Wild Card:** Who is your favorite movie star? If you could ask him or her several questions, what would you ask and why?

☐ **Free Choice**

Developing Writing Fluency © 2000 Creative Teaching Press

Author _____ Week Beginning _____

World of Wonder

Critical Components of Scientific Writing

- Use accurate, detailed, firsthand observations.
- Include focused questions about nature.
- Include hypotheses (educated guesses about your questions).
- Add detailed procedures to test hypotheses.

☐ Think about rain. Record everything you know firsthand about rain and some of your questions about rain. Write your hypotheses. Write detailed procedures for an experiment to test one of your hypotheses.

☐ Think about light. Record what you know about light through observation. Write down your questions and hypotheses about light. Write a test for your hypotheses.

☐ What do you know about the wind? Write down everything you have observed about wind and breezes, hurricanes, and tornadoes. Only record what you have observed firsthand. What questions do you have? What hypotheses do you have about these questions? How could you test these hypotheses?

☐ Think about your favorite animal—mammal, fish, insect, or arachnid. Record every interesting observation you have of this animal. How could you find out the answers to your questions without hurting the animal? What hypotheses do you have? Describe your detailed procedure.

☐ Think about your favorite plant—a rosebush, an apple tree, a cornstalk, or a cactus. Record all your observations about the plant's life cycle, needs, anatomy, growth, flowers, and/or fruits. Write out how you might explore the answers to your questions through experimental design.

☐ What question do you have about nature that is unanswered? What do you know already through observation? What is your hypothesis? How could you test this hypothesis? Explain the procedure you might use.

☐ **Wild Card:** If you had a million dollars, what gifts would you buy for your family and friends? List each person and some of the gifts you would want to buy for him or her and why. For example:

Person	Gift	Why
Mom	new dishwasher	I wouldn't have to help with dishes.

☐ **Free Choice**

Developing Writing Fluency © 2000 Creative Teaching Press

50 — Informative Writing

The Persuasive Writing Domain

The persuasive writing domain has several pages of writing prompts that focus on foundational concepts, such as arguments and propaganda techniques (e.g., bandwagon, plain folks). It then moves into persuasive writing products, such as letters of concern and commercials.

Student Background Knowledge

Oftentimes standardized writing requirements ask little in the area of the persuasive writing domain. Yet, this domain is often the area in which students have the most experience, considering television, movies, videos, and radio, although they may lack skills to create an effective persuasive piece. Ads in these audio sources create a knowledge bank. Additionally, print media, such as billboards and magazine and newspaper ads, add to this bank. You will be surprised by how easily you can tap into students' experiences in this domain.

Career Application

Clearly, the persuasive writing domain draws upon the life experiences of our students. Additionally, because our society is so media oriented, skill in the area of persuasive writing lends itself well to a variety of career paths, including politics, journalism, and advertising. The wise teacher helps students refine their persuasive writing techniques because this is a skill that will serve them well for a lifetime.

Making the Most of the Writing Process

Creatively incorporate your persuasive writing across the curriculum. For example, if your class is studying the gold rush, have students write want ads for jobs or advertisements to sell gold mining tools. Or, if your students are studying science, incorporate persuasive essays about conservation issues. Or, when students are reading literature, have them write a letter of concern from one character to another.

For more fun, invite students and parents to bring in small but highly interesting objects (e.g., small pinecone, toy car, tiny clock). Collect the objects, and group them into boxes labeled *Writing Project Objects*. If you have 60 objects, then every student has 60 potential writing assignments. Vary the assignments to fit the emphasized skills, and invite students to self-select the objects to promote interest. Each object can be used over and over, increasing your potential writing prompts to the hundreds and thousands. For example, if a student writes about the tiny clock, he or she could

- Write a magazine advertisement for the product.
- Write a persuasive letter to the company president promoting the discontinuation of the product.
- Write a television commercial promoting the product, using at least two propaganda techniques (e.g., celebrity endorsement, glittering generalities).

Pros and Cons
Critical Components of Arguments

- Explain why a person believes something.
- Support the explanation with specific facts.
- Address opposing point of view.

☐ Consider one suggested policy change that might make our school safer. List the pros and cons of establishing this new rule. Make a chart about the arguments on both sides and support them with facts. Use this information to write a persuasive essay.

☐ Some people think legalizing drugs would lower crime because people would not have to steal to get the drugs. Do you agree? List several arguments on both sides. Then, write a paragraph about each argument.

☐ Should regular citizens be allowed to have guns in their home? Some people say *yes* and others say *no*. Describe arguments on both sides and provide supporting evidence for each side's opinion.

☐ Some students study at home instead of at school. What do you think about this idea? Describe two or three arguments for and against home schooling.

☐ Some people think middle school (or junior high) should consist of grades 6–8, others think 7–9, and still others prefer only grades 7–8. What kind of configuration do you prefer for the "middle years" and why? List several arguments supporting your viewpoint and then several from the opposing point of view.

☐ Many people enjoy hunting, while others are adamantly opposed. List arguments on both sides. Explain these arguments and support them with facts.

☐ **Wild Card:** Your three-year-old brother never stops moving, laughing, jumping around, wrestling, and being silly. Design a toy that will keep him busy and active all day long and provide some rest and relief for you and your parents. Name the toy, describe how it works, and tell where you will keep it.

☐ **Free Choice**

Author _____ Week Beginning _____

The Art of Persuasion
Critical Components of Persuasive Essays

- Introduction—begin with an interesting lead and a thesis statement that summarizes the main arguments of your opinion.

- Body—include a paragraph for each argument supported by facts and examples. Carefully order body paragraphs with the weakest point in the middle and the strongest at the end.

- Conclusion—include a closing paragraph that restates the main arguments.

☐ Caring for our environment is important to the survival of future generations. Choose one particular area (e.g., air quality, ocean cleanliness, rain forest preservation) and convince your readers of the importance of preserving this aspect of our environment.

☐ Write a persuasive essay to convince your parents you need an allowance or to convince your parents that you should have a raise in allowance.

☐ Think about something you want to change about your school to make it better. Write a persuasive essay convincing your principal and teacher(s) that your idea would work and that it would be good for the students.

☐ The Greeks held the first Olympics more than two and a half centuries ago. In your opinion, what is the most important Olympic event or tradition? Write a persuasive essay to convince your readers.

☐ What is the most important thing a student should learn while growing up? Write a persuasive essay to convince parents and teachers about passing this information along to the next generation.

☐ Think about your neighborhood and city. What would you do to improve it? For example, maybe you need a library or a place kids can go when they are having trouble with something (e.g., homework) or someone (e.g., friends or family). Decide what idea you would like to propose and write a persuasive essay to convince other people to act on it.

☐ **Wild Card:** The year is 3000. There are no places left on earth to build houses. People decide they will build homes over and underneath the oceans. Design a house or neighborhood and describe how all the essentials will be provided: air, land, space, food, plumbing, electricity, and so forth.

☐ **Free Choice**

Greener Grass
Critical Components of Glittering Generalities

- Support an argument for a cause or a product.

- Connect your argument with something everyone recognizes as desirable (e.g., *Shannon's Shampoo makes your hair shine*).

☐ Brainstorm a list of products (e.g., June's Jump Ropes, Richard's Race Cars). Write glittering generalities to support arguments for each product.

☐ Brainstorm a list of desirable character traits (e.g., kindness, respect, responsibility). Create a list of "Prescriptions for Success" that include glittering generalities that show the value of these character traits.

☐ Brainstorm a list of cars and benefits everyone agrees go with each car (e.g., speed, dependability, status). Write glittering generalities for each car.

☐ Brainstorm a list of healthy habits and benefits everyone agrees go with the habits (e.g., brushing teeth: *strong teeth, bright smile*). Write statements with glittering generalities for each healthy habit.

☐ List a number of famous athletes and desirable character traits (e.g., Michael Jordan, agility; Michelle Kwan, grace; Andre Agassi, strength). Convince your readers that they will gain these traits if they only follow your advice.

☐ Consider one thing you want to convince your reader about—perhaps that students should be paid to go to school, parents should not have to work so much, or every student should have his or her own bedroom. Then, create three arguments for that cause and create glittering generalities to support your arguments.

☐ **Wild Card:** Gary Paulsen's *Hatchet* and Will Hobbs' *Far North* both have plane crashes and teenagers who survive in the Canadian wilderness. Imagine that you and your best friend have just crashed in the Canadian wilderness in the dead of winter. Write a story about your crash and how you survived for three long months.

☐ **Free Choice**

Developing Writing Fluency © 2000 Creative Teaching Press

Author _____ Week Beginning _____

Climb Aboard
Critical Components of Bandwagon

- Support an argument for a cause or a product.

- Connect your argument with the audience's desire not to be left out (e.g., *People everywhere are buying Geoffrey's Jammers*).

☐ List ten school items (e.g., *backpacks, rulers, binders*) and use the bandwagon concept to write a sentence for each that convinces your readers to buy the item (e.g., *The majority of eighth graders across the Americas use Bartholomew's Backpacks, the most efficiently organized backpack on the market*).

☐ Most people locate their business at home, in a traditional high-rise office building, in a mall, or in a cluster of smaller business buildings. Design some new creative office space locations (e.g., barges on rivers, tree houses in forests). Describe your new creative locations and convince your readers to consider renting office space at one of them. Incorporate bandwagon concepts in your descriptions.

☐ Design three new styles of houses, such as "Wacky Wing Houses" located in trees and atop windmills or "Close Quarter Houses" located underground or dug into mountainsides. Describe one of your houses and use bandwagon strategies to convince your readers to buy it.

☐ Pretend you are the owner of a factory that produces new, creative, futuristic food items (e.g., sandwiches with handles). Write paragraphs to convince your readers to try out these new foods. Use bandwagon concepts to underscore the advantages of these products over traditional ones.

☐ List your top six favorite videos or movies of all time. Use bandwagon appeals to convince others to see these movies.

☐ Students often tire of traditional school, so create a new one! Have your school out on a field, in the backcountry, on another planet, in the ocean, or on a ski slope. Describe your school and convince your readers that this school is for them. Incorporate bandwagon strategies in your description.

☐ **Wild Card:** School just got cancelled for a year and you just won the lottery. Plan your life for the next twelve months.

☐ **Free Choice**

Plain Folks

Critical Components of Plain Folks

- Support an argument for a cause or a product.

- Connect an issue or a product with common people and common needs (e.g., *Nathaniel Hetzel works hard at school all day long. Only the Bradford Binder will suit his academic needs*).

☐ List five essential farm tools (real or imaginary). Give them creative names. Write a sentence or two for each, using the plain folks technique to convince your readers that these tools are essential for the common farmer.

☐ List five pieces of sports gear for a particular sport. Provide a creative name for each piece. Write a sentence or two for each piece, using the plain folks technique to convince ordinary athletes that these tools are essential for them.

☐ List five kitchen gadgets with creative names. Write a paragraph for each gadget. Use the plain folks technique to convince housewives and househusbands that they need these tools and that ordinary people who care for their homes use the tools.

☐ Abraham Lincoln was "common folk." In *Lincoln on Leadership,* Donald T. Phillips addresses effective strategies Lincoln used to lead the American people. The first strategy was to get out of the office and circulate among the troops. Think about an effective political leader, past or present. Describe his or her traits and use the plain folks strategy to convince voters that these characteristics are valuable in this particular political candidate.

☐ Gary Soto, author of *Baseball in April,* writes books for young readers. Growing up, however, he lived an ordinary childhood in a modern day Mexican American neighborhood in Fresno, California. Think about the ordinary experiences that bring you great pleasure (e.g., playing baseball, riding a bike). List these ordinary experiences and the products that help make them happen (e.g., *baseball, bat, bike*). Write ads, using the plain folks technique, to convince parents that their children need these things.

☐ You own a garden store and sell a line of fruit and vegetable seeds. Write ads, using the plain folks strategy, to convince customers to buy your seeds.

☐ **Wild Card:** Write a story about an elephant who swam across the ocean to escape a cruel master.

☐ **Free Choice**

Hollywood, Here We Come!

Critical Components of Celebrity Endorsement

- Support an argument for a cause or a product.

- Connect an issue or a product with a respected organization or well-known person (e.g., *Michelle Kwan, famous for her energy and enthusiasm on ice, credits her superb health to Campbell's Soup*).

☐ Ansel Adams, respected American photographer, is famous for his black and white photographs of Yosemite National Park. A conservationist at heart, he longed to see nature preserved. Think about something in nature you want to preserve. Write a paragraph arguing for its preservation. Include a celebrity endorsement.

☐ C. S. Lewis, author of *The Lion, the Witch, and the Wardrobe,* promoted honesty and obedience through the main characters' victories. Record some important character qualities. Write a brief story for each, emphasizing the trait's importance. Include celebrities or characters who exemplify (serve as an example for) the trait.

☐ Who do you think has the most fabulous hair (e.g., healthy hair, sheen, great style, unusual length or color)? Use this person as a celebrity endorsement in an ad for a hair product.

☐ Who do you know that is an excellent student? Invent an imaginary product that makes him or her successful. Use your friend as the celebrity endorsement to advertise the product.

☐ In 1984, Theodore Geisel, otherwise known as Dr. Seuss, received a special award from the Pulitzer Prize Committee for his lifetime of contributions to children's literature. Select a Dr. Seuss book and use another author as a celebrity endorsement to advertise the book to a parent audience.

☐ Who do you know that has a fabulous smile? Invent an imaginary product that contributes to his or her great smile (e.g., Dazzle White Toothpaste, Grinning Gooze, Magic Teeth Straightener). Write text for an ad to convince others to buy the product. Use your friend as a celebrity endorsement.

☐ **Wild Card:** What kind of car would you like? Lamborghini? Porsche? Mercedes Benz? Imagine the car is yours for one week. Where will you go? What will you do? Who will go with you? Describe the car and your wild adventure.

☐ **Free Choice**

Developing Writing Fluency © 2000 Creative Teaching Press

Persuasive Writing

Unbelievable
Critical Components of Loaded Words

- Support an argument for a cause or a product.
- Use words or phrases that have strong emotional impact (e.g., *GermFree Baby Lotion **kills deadly diseases** before they happen, **protecting the life** of your infant*).

☐ List six medical products in your home. Choose one medical product that is extremely important (e.g., bacterial soap, gauze, thermometer). Write a paragraph telling your readers why they must buy this product and keep it handy at home. Use loaded words in your explanation.

☐ List five pieces of essential gardening equipment, sports equipment, computer equipment, or household tools. Write a magazine piece, highlighting three products in one category. Use loaded words to promote your product line.

☐ Create a list of your "Top Ten" favorite videos. Then, narrow the list to two or three videos that every person *must* see! Write a commercial advertising each video, incorporating loaded words to convince the viewers.

☐ Artists require special tools (e.g., brushes, paints, canvases). Invent products to assist artists. Use loaded words in advertisements that promote the products.

☐ *Prevention* magazine features articles about healthy living. Articles highlight natural remedies, such as green tea, exercise, and nutritious foods. Write a promotional flyer designed to convince your readers that, in order to live healthy lives, they must subscribe to *Prevention* magazine.

☐ University of California at Irvine has conducted studies that indicate listening to certain types of music (e.g., Bach's sonatas) can actually boost your performance on standardized tests. What types of music do you enjoy? How does music help you? Write a convincing essay, persuading the school to play this music over loudspeakers in your class. Use loaded words to convince school personnel.

☐ **Wild Card:** Write a story about the best thing that ever happened to you, the funniest thing that ever happened to you, or the most mysterious thing that ever happened to you.

☐ **Free Choice**

Developing Writing Fluency © 2000 Creative Teaching Press

Author _____ Week Beginning _____

To Whom It May Concern
Critical Components of Letters of Concern

- Begin with the date and a greeting.
- Open with a positive statement.
- Include a "however" statement that leads into a concern.
- Suggest an action plan and the benefits of this plan.
- End with a positive closing.

☐ Write a letter of concern to the president of the United States about any issue that is of concern to you.

☐ Write a letter of concern to your school principal, describing what is right about your school and an area you would like to see improved. Remember to suggest a plan of action that is reasonable and positive.

☐ You are the boss of an oil company. Most of your employees are hard workers; however, there is an employee who, though she works hard, is rude to customers on the phone. Write a letter of concern, describing what is good and bad about her work performance. Suggest ways for her to improve.

☐ Write a letter to yourself, commending yourself for what you have been doing well and addressing an area of concern. Do not forget the action plan and be merciful!

☐ Write a letter to your best friend, describing what is going well in your relationship and an area you would like to see improve.

☐ It is 15 years from now and you are an experienced sixth-grade teacher. You have a brilliant student in your classroom, but this student never gets his work in on time and when he does, it is often messily written. Write the student and his parents a letter of concern. Remember to start with the positive before you bring up the negative. Also, make practical suggestions for an action plan to improve performance.

☐ **Wild Card:** You have just turned into a banana, a grape, or an orange. Choose one and tell your life story—from beginning to end!

☐ **Free Choice**

Vote for Me!

Critical Components of Campaign Speeches

- State an opinion and attempt to persuade.

- Introduction—begin with an interesting lead and a thesis statement.

- Body—include a paragraph for each reason supported by facts and examples.

- Conclusion—include a brief restatement of the main idea.

- Use persuasive language techniques (e.g., loaded words, bandwagon).

☐ Four-star General Colin Powell was raised in the South Bronx, grew up in a supportive family, worked hard to move up, and succeeded in the military. Powell talks unselfconsciously about race. "How did I deal with racism?" he asked rhetorically. "I beat it. I said, 'I am not going to carry this burden of racism. I'm going to destroy your stereotype. I'm proud to be black. You carry this burden of racism, because I'm not going to.'" How would his background uniquely qualify him to meet the needs of the people he represents? Write a presidential campaign speech for Colin Powell.

☐ Your neighborhood needs someone to be the "Neighborhood Leader." The Neighborhood Leader will plan meetings and parties, clean up, and help with safety issues and childcare issues. You do not really want the job, but the only other person who is running is involved in gangs. You decide you have to run for the position to save your neighborhood. Write the most convincing, persuasive speech possible.

☐ You are running for school president, school secretary, or school treasurer. Choose the job that best suits your talents. Write a campaign speech telling why you are the best man or woman for the job.

☐ Someone in your family is running for governor of your state. This person asks you to help write the speech. Carefully organize the speech to convince the listeners of his or her qualifications.

☐ Write a campaign speech to become the president of a space station outside our solar system.

☐ Write a campaign speech to become the president of your local veterinary hospital, library board, or children's hospital.

☐ **Wild Card:** Invent a silent game. What is the name of the game? How do you play it?

☐ **Free Choice**

Media Mania

Critical Components of Commercials

- Invent a clever, memorable name for the product.

- Describe the special features of the product.

- Use persuasive language and techniques (e.g., celebrity endorsement, bandwagon).

- Establish a sense of urgency to purchase the product.

- Write in script style, including descriptions of actions, gestures, props, and scenes.

☐ Imagine a machine that will provide a pollution-free source of electricity. Write a commercial to advertise this product.

☐ Imagine a car that both drives and flies. What does it look like? What types of special features does it have? Write a commercial to convince your readers that the car is a worthy investment.

☐ Many people have problems with "pests," such as termites, killer bees, red ants, mosquitoes, and locusts. Choose one of these pesky pests and imagine a product that helps get rid of them. Write a convincing commercial for the product.

☐ We regularly see shocking commercials intended to convince people to stay off drugs. Write a tasteful commercial that will benefit young viewers, convincing them not to take drugs or alcohol. Incorporate in your commercial what they can do instead (e.g., stay in school, get involved with sports).

☐ The world's rain forests are being cut down at an alarming rate. We are unable to plant trees and grow them fast enough to replace dwindling forests. How can we reduce wood and paper consumption? Write a compelling commercial script about a product and/or habit that would contribute to saving our world's forests.

☐ If you could redesign your community, neighborhood, or city, what would you do? How would you change it? Write out your plan and then a commercial to convince others to participate.

☐ **Wild Card:** You are a zookeeper. Last night there was an earthquake and twelve animals escaped. Describe the events of the night from an escaped animal's point of view.

☐ **Free Choice**

Author _____ Week Beginning _____

Buy now!
Critical Components of Advertisements

- Give the product a clever, memorable name.
- Describe the special features of the product.
- Use persuasive words and phrases.
- Establish a sense of urgency to purchase the product.
- Make it clear that the product is affordable.
- Include a graphic layout sketch, suggestions for visual impact, and potential places for advertisements (e.g., magazines, newspapers, billboards).

☐ Create a magazine advertisement for nail polish. Include illustrations for the ad.

☐ Write a magazine advertisement for your favorite doll, model car, or game. Include illustrations for the ad.

☐ Make a newspaper ad for a special sale at your local clothing store. Convince your community to come.

☐ Write a newspaper advertisement for the local public or private school you have just started. Highlight the best aspects of the school and why parents should enroll their children. Indicate school hours, classroom design, quality of teachers, playground and building facilities, extracurricular activities, and costs.

☐ Write an advertisement for a travel magazine to convince people to travel to your city.

☐ A mad but brilliant scientist has just invented a machine that will turn you into any kind of animal for up to a week. This means you could learn what it is like to live as a tarantula, dinosaur, horse, or whale. The only problem is that the scientist cannot completely guarantee your safety; however, the last 100 people to try his machine have returned safely. People are paying exorbitant (extreme) prices for the experience. Write a magazine article to convince people to try it out, but honestly caution them about the possible risks.

☐ **Wild Card:** Watch out! You have just been shrunk and are now living the life of a leprechaun, a gnome, or an elf. Where do you live? What are you doing with your life? What kinds of problems do you have? What are your wishes?

☐ **Free Choice**

Help Wanted

Critical Components of Want Ads

- Describe the type of job.

- Include the job description (duties).

- Tell the experience and skills required.

- Tell the compensation (e.g., hourly or salary wage, benefits).

- End with the name of the company and contact information (e.g., address or telephone).

☐ You are Captain Nemo of the submarine Nautilus featured in Jules Verne's *20,000 Leagues Under the Sea*. You are in need of some excellent marines for a three-month voyage. Write the ads for the positions you need to fill.

☐ You are in charge of the county fair this coming summer. List the jobs that will be available. Choose five of the jobs and write want ads for them.

☐ In Disney's *Mary Poppins,* the father and his children have very different ideas about the kind of nanny they want to employ. The father uses words such as "firm, respectable, and no-nonsense." The children want someone "witty, very sweet, and fairly pretty." Imagine your parents are going on an extended vacation and leaving you at home. Write a want ad to attract the ideal person to care for you in their absence. Be sure to list experience needed, duties to be performed, and compensation.

☐ Hire a classroom assistant for your teacher. What qualifications would such a person need to help you? To help your teacher?

☐ You are the president of the United States. Write want ads for three key positions you want to fill with people you handpick.

☐ Create a want ad for a manager of a space station. Be sure to identify desirable qualifications and length of service needed.

☐ **Wild Card:** You have been invited to travel around the world in 80 days with Phileas Fogg. You will travel by boat, train, hot-air balloon, and a variety of other modes of transportation. Describe your adventures as you cross the continents and oceans.

☐ **Free Choice**

Author _____ Week Beginning _____

Dear Editor
Critical Components of Editorials

- Begin with a greeting (e.g., *Dear Editor*).
- Address a recent article or current concern in the opening line.
- Express an opinion and reasons and examples to support it.
- Restate concern with a call for action in the closing paragraph.

☐ A law has just passed that every young man and woman, after graduating from high school, will be required to serve one year in the armed services. You will be paid for your services and you may continue your military career beyond a year if you are successful. However, you do not have the option of attending college for at least one year until you have completed your community service in the military. What do you think about this law? Write your local editor and tell him or her your opinions.

☐ Today you read a newspaper article that said a young man was shot and killed by a stray bullet while walking to your school. You are extremely upset by this incident. Write a letter to the local paper, stating what it feels like to be a young, unprotected pedestrian (someone who goes places on foot).

☐ You pick up the paper and read that your school is now requiring you to wear uniforms. Write the editor of the local newspaper and tell him or her what you think.

☐ A law has just passed outlawing cats and dogs from living in your town because they are a health menace. Write the local editor and express your opinion on the matter.

☐ In the past, some cities have sprayed malathion, a strong pesticide, over the entire city during the night. You have just read that your city is going to do the same. The city council has told community members to stay indoors. Write your local editor and tell him or her what you are thinking.

☐ Over 40 people in your neighborhood reported an unidentified flying object on the same night years ago. This sighting had been kept secret, but hit the front headlines this morning. Write your local editor and tell what you think about these UFO sightings.

☐ **Wild Card:** Who is your favorite sports figure? If you could ask him or her five questions, what would they be and why?

☐ **Free Choice**